SCHOLASTIC

Reading Passages
That Build Comprehension

COMPARE & CONTRAST

BY LINDA WARD BEECH

☆ ☆ ☆

NEW YORK • TORONTO • LONDON • AUCKLAND • SYDNEY
MEXICO CITY • NEW DELHI • HONG KONG • BUENOS AIRES

Teaching *Resources*

Contents

Cover design by Maria Lilja
Interior design by Holly Grundon
Interior art by Mike Gordon

ISBN 0-439-55427-6
Copyright © 2005 by Linda Ward Beech.
All rights reserved.
Printed in the U.S.A.

2 3 4 5 6 7 8 9 10   40   14 13 12 11 10 09 08 07 06

Introduction

R eading comprehension involves numerous thinking skills. Making comparisons is one such skill. A reader who can compare and contrast events, characters, places, and facts gains a richer understanding of a text. This book will help you help students learn to compare and contrast. Use the pages that follow to teach this skill to students and to give them practice in employing it.

Using This Book

Pages 5-7

After introducing comparing and contrasting to students (see page 4), duplicate and pass out pages 5–7. Use page 5 to help students review and practice what they have just learned about comparing and contrasting. By explaining their thinking, students are using metacognition to analyze how they found similarities and differences. Pages 6–7 give students a model of the practice pages to come. They also provide a model of the thinking students might use in comparing and contrasting.

Page 8

Use this page as a pre-assessment to find out how students think when they compare and contrast. When going over these pages with students, be sure they understand that a comparison shows similarities. A contrast shows differences.

Pages 9-43

These pages offer practice in comparing and contrasting. Students should first read the paragraph and then answer the questions. The first question on each page asks students to identify a similarity, while the second question focuses on a difference. Students should fill in the bubble in front of the correct answer, based on the paragraph. They are then asked to identify and write another similarity or difference from the paragraph. Encourage students to write a complete sentence for item 3 on each page.

Pages 44-46

After they have completed the practice pages, use these pages to assess the way students think when they compare and contrast.

Page 47

You may wish to keep a record of students' progress as they complete the practice pages. Sample comments that will help you guide students toward improving their skills might include:
- reads carelessly
- misunderstands text
- fails to observe and identify similarities or differences
- doesn't apply prior knowledge
- lacks background to compare and contrast

Teacher Tip

For students who need extra help, you might suggest that they keep pages 5–7 with them to use as examples when they complete the practice pages.

Mini-Lesson: Teaching About Comparing & Contrasting

1. Introduce the concept: Display a peach and an orange. Then write these statements on the chalkboard:

The peach and orange are alike.

The peach and orange are different.

Ask students to tell you one way that the peach and orange are alike. Then have them tell how the two pieces of fruit are different.

2. Model thinking: After students have identified ways in which the peach and orange are alike and different, continue the lesson by modeling how students might think aloud.

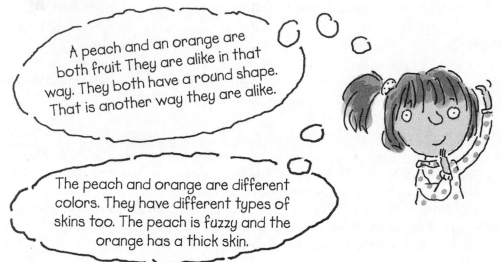

A peach and an orange are both fruit. They are alike in that way. They both have a round shape. That is another way they are alike.

The peach and orange are different colors. They have different types of skins too. The peach is fuzzy and the orange has a thick skin.

Teacher Tip

Students can learn a lot if you review the finished practice pages with them on a regular basis. Encourage students to explain their thinking for each correct answer. Ask them to point out the words that helped them compare and contrast. Discuss why the other sentences are not correct choices.

3. Define the skill: Explain that when you find similarities between two things, you are **comparing** them. When you find differences between things, you are **contrasting** them. Point out that often things have both similarities and differences. Understanding how things are alike and different helps a reader to organize and comprehend information.

Tell students that phrases such as *similar to* and *the same as* are often used in comparing things. Phrases such as *bigger than* or *more colorful than* are often used in contrasting things.

Use a Venn diagram to help students who are visual learners understand the concept.

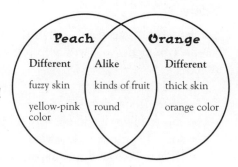

Peach		**Orange**
Different	Alike	Different
fuzzy skin	kinds of fruit	thick skin
yellow-pink color	round	orange color

4. Practice the skill: Use Practice Pages 9–43 to give students practice in comparing and contrasting.

Name_____   Date_____

What Is Comparing? What Is Contrasting?

You read a paragraph. It tells you about two or more things.
This can be confusing. How can a reader sort out this information?
A good reader compares and contrasts things. A reader might think:

How are these things alike?

How do they differ?

When you answer the first question, you are **comparing**. You are finding similarities. When you answer the second question, you are **contrasting**. You are finding differences.

Read the paragraph below, and then answer the questions.

Sharks!

The great white shark lives in deep, cold seas. It will attack large animals such as sea lions. The bull shark lives mostly in shallow waters. It is sometimes found in rivers. These sharks are both very good swimmers and hunters. Both kinds of sharks have lots of teeth too!

This paragraph compares _____

and _____ .

How are the sharks alike?

1. What kind of swimmers are both sharks?

   _____

2. How many teeth do these sharks have?

   _____

How do the sharks differ?

3. Where does the great white shark live?

   _____

4. Where does the bull shark live?

   _____

Name _____ Date _____

Comparing & Contrasting

Study these two pages. They show how a student compared and contrasted.

Read the paragraph. Then fill in the
bubble that best answers each question.

Fox Facts

An animal's home often affects how that animal looks. A fox that lives in the cold Arctic has thick fur. The fur of the Arctic fox is reddish brown in summer but white in winter. A kit fox lives in the desert. There the temperatures are much warmer. The kit fox stays the same light brown color all year. It has bigger ears than an Arctic fox. Both kinds of foxes hunt small animals.

1. How are the foxes alike?

○ A. Their fur changes color in the winter.

Only the fur of the Arctic fox changes color.

○ B. They live in the same kind of climate.

The Arctic is cold, and the desert is warm.

◉ C. They hunt small animals for food.

Yes, both kinds of foxes hunt smaller animals.

I am going to fill in **C**. This sentence tells how the foxes are alike.

Continued ⟶

Comparing & Contrasting

(Continued)

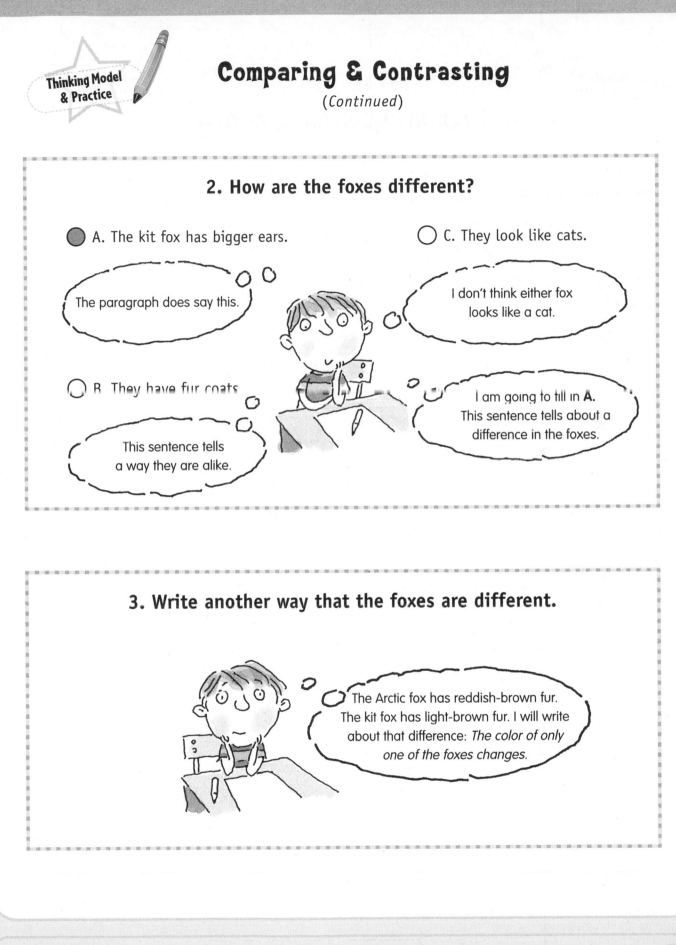

2. How are the foxes different?

● A. The kit fox has bigger ears.

The paragraph does say this.

○ B. They have fur coats.

This sentence tells a way they are alike.

○ C. They look like cats.

I don't think either fox looks like a cat.

I am going to fill in **A.** This sentence tells about a difference in the foxes.

3. Write another way that the foxes are different.

The Arctic fox has reddish-brown fur. The kit fox has light-brown fur. I will write about that difference: *The color of only one of the foxes changes.*

Pre-Assessment Name_____ Date_____

Looking for Similarities and Differences

Study the picture.

Read each sentence.

Make a check ✓ if the sentence tells about both the knife and spoon.

Make an **X** if the sentence tells about only the knife or only the spoon.

_____ 1. They have handles.

_____ 2. They are sharp.

_____ 3. They are for cutting.

_____ 4. They are for eating.

_____ 5. They are for scooping.

_____ 6. They are used in the kitchen.

7. Write a sentence to tell another way that the knife and spoon are similar.

_____

_____

_____

8. Write a sentence to tell another way that the knife and spoon are different.

_____

_____

_____

Name_____ Date _____

Read the paragraph. Then answer the questions.

Meet Two Dogs

Meet Aibo and Fido. Aibo is a dog. But he is also a robot. Aibo is expensive—he costs $2,500. Many people like this metal pet. He comes when he's called, and he doesn't need to be walked. Fido is a mutt, but he's a real dog. His furry coat sometimes sheds. His owner must take him out twice a day. Fido's owner got him for free from an animal shelter. Both Aibo and Fido have learned to do tricks.

1. How are the dogs alike?

○ A. They cost a lot of money.

○ B. They are someone's pets.

○ C. They are both mutts.

2. How are the dogs different?

○ A. Fido can do tricks.

○ B. Aibo is made of metal.

○ C. Aibo needs to be walked.

3. Write another way that the dogs are different.

_____

_____

_____

_____

_____

_____

Practice Page 2

Name_____ Date_____

Read the paragraph. Then answer the questions.

Birds and Turtles

Mother birds lay eggs in nests where they are safe. Little birds hatch from the eggs. They cheep and cheep until their parents bring them food. Turtles lay eggs, too. Mother turtles lay their eggs in the sand where the eggs will be safe. But mother turtles cover the eggs and leave. When it is time, small turtles hatch from the eggs. They dig their way up and learn to find food on their own.

1. **How are birds and turtles alike?**

   ◯ A. They have hard shells.

   ◯ B. The young hatch from eggs.

   ◯ C. The mothers leave the eggs.

2. **How are birds and turtles different?**

   ◯ A. Bird parents feed their young.

   ◯ B. They lay eggs in safe places.

   ◯ C. The young need food to eat.

3. **Write another difference between bird and turtle eggs.**

   _____

   _____

   _____

   _____

   _____

   _____

Practice Page 3

Name_____ Date_____

Read the paragraph. Then answer the questions.

Two Kinds of Cats

Leopards and lions are two kinds of wild cats. Both are big meat eaters that hunt other animals for food. Leopards have thick golden-yellow fur coats covered with dark spots. They are very good climbers. They often take their food up into trees for dinner. Leopards like to be alone. Lions are more than twice the size of leopards. These tan cats live together in groups called prides.

1. How are leopards and lions alike?

   ◯ A. They eat meat.

   ◯ B. They have spots.

   ◯ C. They live in prides.

2. How are leopards and lions different?

   ◯ A. They are hunters.

   ◯ B. Lions are bigger.

   ◯ C. Leopards are cats.

3. Write another way that leopards and lions are alike.

   _____

   _____

   _____

   _____

   _____

   _____

Practice Page 4

Name_____ Date_____

Read the paragraph. Then answer the questions.

Saying "Thank You"

People around the world say "thank you" for many things. Some places have special customs. In Taiwan fishermen set off fireworks. This is how they thank the goddess of the sea. They thank her for protecting them from storms and shipwrecks. In Mexico people who have lived through an accident or illness make *retablos*. These are small paintings on pieces of metal. The retablos are thank-yous from these grateful people.

1. **How are customs in Taiwan and Mexico alike?**

   ○ A. They use fireworks.

   ○ B. They use paintings.

   ○ C. They give thanks.

2. **How are customs in Taiwan and Mexico different?**

   ○ A. Mexicans give thanks for recovering from illness.

   ○ B. People in Taiwan are grateful for something.

   ○ C. People in Mexico have special customs.

3. **Write another way that customs differ in Taiwan and Mexico.**

   _____

   _____

   _____

   _____

   _____

   _____

   _____

Practice Page 5

Name_____ Date_____

Read the paragraph. Then answer the questions.

Which Is It?

Is it a butterfly or a moth? Both belong to the same group of insects. Both have wings and feelers called antennae. But most butterflies hold their wings up when they land. Most moths keep their wings flat. Butterflies are usually active during the day. Moths are usually busy at night. The antennae on a butterfly have knobs on the end. Moths do not have these.

1. How are butterflies and moths alike?

○ A. They have antennae.

○ B. They hold their wings up.

○ C. They are active at night.

2. How are butterflies and moths different?

○ A. Moths don't have knobs on their antennae.

○ B. Butterflies belong to a different insect group.

○ C. Butterflies have bigger wings than moths.

3. Write another way that moths and butterflies are alike.

_____

_____

_____

_____

_____

_____

_____

Name_____ Date_____

Read the paragraph. Then answer the questions.

Surfing

Surfing is a popular sport in oceans and the Great Lakes. It takes a stormy day for good waves to build on the lakes. Usually lake surfers go out in the winter. They wear long wetsuits to keep warm in the cold waters. Ocean surfers can count on good waves much more often. They can usually wear just bathing suits and surf in sunny weather. Surfers use a board for both lake and ocean surfing.

1. How are lake and ocean surfing alike?

○ A. The surfers always wear wetsuits.

○ B. The surfers use a board on the waves.

○ C. The surfers can count on good waves.

2. How are lake and ocean surfing different?

○ A. Lake surfers usually wear bathing suits.

○ B. The sport is popular in both kinds of water.

○ C. Lake waves build only in stormy weather.

3. Write another way that lake and ocean surfing are different.

_____

_____

_____

_____

_____

_____

Practice Page 7 Name_____ Date_____

Read the paragraph. Then answer the questions.

Racing Cars

Have you ever seen a racing car? Formula One cars race on tracks. These are high-powered cars that go very fast. They have specially made bodies and engines. Stock cars are regular cars that have been changed for racing. These cars go fast but not as fast as Formula One racers. Stock cars usually race on tracks too.

1. **How are Formula One cars and stock cars alike?**

   ○ A. They have specially made engines.

   ○ B. They are made from regular cars.

   ○ C. They are used for races on tracks.

2. **How are Formula One cars and stock cars different?**

   ○ A. They use a parachute to stop them.

   ○ B. Formula One racing cars go faster.

   ○ C. Stock cars have specially made bodies.

3. **Write another way that Formula One cars and stock cars are different.**

   _____

   _____

   _____

   _____

   _____

   _____

Practice Page 8

Name_____ Date_____

Read the paragraph. Then answer the questions.

All About Bears

Bears have poor eyesight. They have poor hearing too. Instead, they use their sense of smell to find food. Brown bears are called grizzly bears because of white hairs in their fur. Brown bears eat plants. Sometimes they eat fish or other animals. Polar bears eat only meat. They have white fur and live in the Arctic. Polar bears have special cups on the soles of their feet to keep them from sliding on ice. These bears are bigger than brown bears.

1. How are brown bears and polar bears alike?

○ A. They eat only plants.

○ B. They have white fur.

○ C. They have poor hearing.

2. How are brown bears and polar bears different?

○ A. Polar bears have a good sense of smell.

○ B. Polar bears eat other animals for food.

○ C. Brown bears are called grizzlies.

3. Write another way that brown bears and polar bears are alike.

_____

_____

_____

_____

_____

Practice Page 9

Name_____ Date_____

Read the paragraph. Then answer the questions.

Mercury and Venus

Mercury and Venus are closer to the sun than Earth. However, Mercury is 36 million miles from the sun. Venus is 67 million miles away. It takes Mercury 88 days to orbit the sun. Venus spends about 230 days orbiting once around the sun. Venus is about the same size as Earth. Mercury is much smaller. Both Mercury and Venus get very hot. Scientists do not think there is life on either planet.

Earth

Venus

mercury

SUN

1. **How are Mercury and Venus alike?**

   ◯ A. They are the same size.

   ◯ B. They both orbit the sun.

   ◯ C. Mercury is nearer the sun.

2. **How are Mercury and Venus different?**

   ◯ A. Venus takes longer to orbit the sun.

   ◯ B. There is no life on either planet.

   ◯ C. Mercury is closer to the sun than Earth.

3. **Write another way that Mercury and Venus are alike.**

   _____

   _____

   _____

   _____

   _____

   _____

Practice Page 10

Name_____ Date_____

Read the paragraph. Then answer the questions.

American Colonies

n the early days of the United States, there were 13 colonies. All of them were in the East along the Atlantic Ocean. One colony was New York. It was founded by a Dutchman, Peter Minuit, in 1624. The purpose of this colony was to increase trade for the Dutch. Another colony was Rhode Island. Roger Williams started it in 1636. He wanted people who lived there to have religious freedom.

NY

Rhode Island

New York

1. How were the colonies of New York and Rhode Island alike?

   ○ A. They were founded by the Dutch.

   ○ B. They were along the Atlantic Ocean.

   ○ C. They were started in 1636.

2. How were the colonies of New York and Rhode Island different?

   ○ A. They were among the first 13 American colonies.

   ○ B. New York was started for religious freedom.

   ○ C. Rhode Island was founded by Roger Williams.

3. Write another way the colonies of New York and Rhode Island were different.

   _____

   _____

   _____

   _____

   _____

   _____

Practice Page 11 Name_____ Date_____

Read the paragraph. Then answer the questions.

Looking at Leaves

The leaves on trees are not all alike. Some leaves have jagged edges called teeth. Toothed leaves can be oval, skinny, or shaped like a heart. Beech and elm trees have such leaves. Other trees have leaves shaped like a hand with the fingers spread out. These leaves have three to seven fingers or lobes. Many maple trees have such leaves. Both types of leaves drop off trees in the fall.

1. **How are toothed leaves and hand-shaped leaves alike?**

   ○ A. They grow on trees.

   ○ B. They have lobes.

   ○ C. They have teeth.

2. **How are toothed leaves and hand-shaped leaves different?**

   ○ A. Maple leaves drop off in the fall.

   ○ B. Elm leaves are shaped like hands.

   ○ C. Toothed leaves have jagged edges.

3. **Write another way that toothed leaves and hand-shaped leaves are different.**

   _____

   _____

   _____

   _____

   _____

Name_____ Date_____

Read the paragraph. Then answer the questions.

The Carolinas

Two U.S. states share the name Carolina. Both states are on the Atlantic Ocean. North Carolina is bigger and has more people. It became the twelfth state in 1789. The first successful airplane flight took place in North Carolina. The capital is Raleigh. South Carolina became the eighth state in 1788. Its capital is Columbia. North and South Carolina are in the South.

1. How are North and South Carolina alike?

○ A. They are on the Atlantic Ocean.

○ B. Raleigh is the capital city.

○ C. They have the same population.

2. How are North and South Carolina different?

○ A. South Carolina is in the South.

○ B. They became states together.

○ C. North Carolina is larger.

3. Write another way that North and South Carolina are alike.

_____

_____

_____

_____

_____

Practice Page 13

Name_____ Date_____

Read the paragraph. Then answer the questions.

Play Ball

Baseball and basketball are both played with balls. In baseball the players hit the ball with a bat. In basketball the players toss the ball through a hoop. Both sports are played with teams. A basketball team has five players, while a baseball team has nine. In baseball the way to score is to get runs. Basketball players try to get goals. In both sports the team with the higher score wins.

1. **How are baseball and basketball alike?**

   ○ A. They have five players.

   ○ B. They are team sports.

   ○ C. The ball goes through a hoop.

2. **How are baseball and basketball different?**

   ○ A. The highest scoring team wins.

   ○ B. Baseball players hit the ball with a bat.

   ○ C. Basketball is played with a ball.

3. **Write another way that baseball and basketball are different.**

   _____

   _____

   _____

   _____

   _____

Practice Page **14**

Name_____ Date_____

Read the paragraph. Then answer the questions.

Apple Facts

Apples all grow on trees, but they are not the same. A Cortland apple is bright red with green streaks. It is quite juicy. Cortlands are good for eating fresh and for cooking. People often use them in salads too. Another red apple is the Red Delicious. It too has green streaks. The Red Delicious apple is heart-shaped and has five knobs on the bottom. People eat this apple fresh.

1. **How are Cortland and Red Delicious apples alike?**

   ○ A. They are used for cooking.

   ○ B. They are heart-shaped.

   ○ C. They are red in color.

2. **How are Cortland and Red Delicious apples different?**

   ○ A. The Red Delicious apple is heart-shaped.

   ○ B. The Cortland apple is eaten fresh.

   ○ C. The Red Delicious apple has green streaks.

3. **Write another way that the Cortland and Delicious apples are alike.**

   _____

   _____

   _____

   _____

   _____

Practice Page 15   Name_____   Date_____

Read the paragraph. Then answer the questions.

Stormy Weather

Both cyclones and blizzards are dangerous storms. Cyclones usually start near the equator, where the ocean is warm. A cyclone is a spinning storm with heavy rain and raging winds. The winds can rip off roofs and flatten buildings. A blizzard is a snowstorm. It also has strong winds that blow snow into huge piles. Blizzards can cause pipes to freeze, power lines to break, and buildings to fall.

1. **How are cyclones and blizzards alike?**

   ◯ A. They are strong snowstorms.

   ◯ B. They start near the equator.

   ◯ C. They have powerful winds.

2. **How are cyclones and blizzards different?**

   ◯ A. They destroy buildings.

   ◯ B. Cyclones have heavy rain.

   ◯ C. Blizzards are desert storms.

3. **Write another way that cyclones and blizzards are different.**

   _____

   _____

   _____

   _____

   _____

Name_____ Date_____

Read the paragraph. Then answer the questions.

All Aboard

Some people enjoy traveling by train. The Blue Train in South Africa is pulled by an electric engine. This train gives passengers a first-class trip. There are sleeping cabins and a dining car. Another first-class train is the Canadian. It crosses Canada. Passengers can also sleep and eat on this train. The Canadian is pulled by diesel engines. Watching the scenery is popular on both trains.

1. How are the Blue Train and the Canadian alike?

   ○ A. They offer first-class trips.

   ○ B. They are pulled by diesels.

   ○ C. They are in South Africa.

2. How are the Blue Train and the Canadian different?

   ○ A. Passengers can sleep on the Canadian.

   ○ B. The Blue Train is pulled by an electric engine.

   ○ C. People enjoy traveling on the Blue Train.

3. Write another way that the Blue Train and the Canadian are alike.

   _____

   _____

   _____

   _____

   _____

   _____

Practice Page 17 Name_____ Date_____

Read the paragraph. Then answer the questions.

Reading About Rocks

Rocks are millions of years old. Quartz is a hard rock. Some pieces of quartz are used to make jewelry or marbles. Quartz is an igneous rock. That means it comes from the lava of a volcano. Another type of rock is limestone. This rock is formed from the shells of long-ago animals. It is known as sedimentary rock. Chalk is made of limestone. This rock is also used in cement.

1. How are quartz and limestone alike?

   ○ A. They are from volcano lava.

   ○ B. They are sedimentary rocks.

   ○ C. People use them to make things.

2. How are quartz and limestone different?

   ○ A. They are millions of years old.

   ○ B. Quartz is used to make chalk.

   ○ C. Quartz is an igneous rock.

3. Write another way that quartz and limestone are different.

   _____

   _____

   _____

   _____

   _____

   _____

Practice Page 18

Name_____ Date_____

Read the paragraph. Then answer the questions.

Strange Creatures

People tell of strange creatures. One is Sasquatch. Reports of this furry, apelike creature come from forests in North America. Explorers have seen large footprints that might belong to Sasquatch. Another creature is the Yeti. It is also hairy and apelike. The Yeti is said to live in the Himalayas near Tibet and Nepal. People there say they too have seen footprints. No real proof of these creatures has been found.

1. **How are Sasquatch and the Yeti alike?**

   ○ A. They are apelike creatures.

   ○ B. They live in North America.

   ○ C. Scientists say they are real.

2. **How are Sasquatch and the Yeti different?**

   ○ A. The Yeti is said to live near Tibet.

   ○ B. People have reported footprints.

   ○ C. Sasquatch is a hairy animal.

3. **Write another way that Sasquatch and the Yeti are alike.**

   _____

   _____

   _____

   _____

   _____

Practice Page 19

Name_____ Date_____

Read the paragraph. Then answer the questions.

Frogs and Toads

People often confuse frogs and toads. Both are amphibians. This means they are cold-blooded; their temperature stays the same as their surroundings. Frogs and toads have four legs and no tails. They use their back legs for jumping. The legs on frogs are longer. Toads have drier, lumpier skin. Most adult frogs live in or near water. Most adult toads live on land.

1. How are frogs and toads alike?

○ A. They live mostly on land.

○ B. They are cold-blooded.

○ C. They have long tails.

2. How are frogs and toads different?

○ A. Toads jump with their back legs.

○ B. Toads live mostly on land.

○ C. Frogs have lumpier skin.

3. Write another way that frogs and toads are alike.

_____

_____

_____

_____

_____

_____

Practice Page 20   Name_____   Date_____

Read the paragraph. Then answer the questions.

Summer Months

For most students, July and August are summer vacation months. Both of these months are named after Roman emperors. Both months have 31 days. July is the seventh month of the year, and August is the eighth. July has one of our nation's biggest holidays, Independence Day. August is not a month of national holidays. However, P. L. Travers was born in August. She wrote the Mary Poppins books.

1. **How are July and August alike?**

   ○ A. They are vacation months.

   ○ B. They have national holidays.

   ○ C. They are winter months.

2. **How are July and August different?**

   ○ A. August is named for a Roman emperor.

   ○ B. Independence Day falls in July.

   ○ C. August has a total of 31 days.

3. **Write another way that July and August are different.**

   _____

   _____

   _____

   _____

   _____

   _____

Name_____ Date_____

Read the paragraph. Then answer the questions.

Police Talk

Police officers in many cities have a special language. For example, a suspect in New York City is called a perp. In Chicago a suspect is an offender. Police in both cities wear a badge. It is called a tin in New York and a button in Chicago. When someone is arrested in New York, it is called a collar. In Chicago it is a pinch. What do the police call a squad car? In New York it is an R.M.P. The same thing is called a flivver in Chicago.

1. How is police talk in New York City and Chicago the same?

○ A. They call an arrest a collar.

○ B. They call a badge a button.

○ C. They both have names for squad cars.

2. How is police talk in New York City and Chicago different?

○ A. In New York a suspect is called a special name.

○ B. In Chicago a squad car is called a flivver.

○ C. In Chicago the police officers wear a badge.

3. Write another way that police talk is different in New York City and Chicago.

_____

_____

_____

_____

_____

_____

Practice Page 22   Name_____   Date_____

Read the paragraph. Then answer the questions.

Whale Tales

Whales live all their lives in water. These large mammals are very smart. The blue whale is the biggest mammal of all. Both it and the humpback whale are baleen whales. They have no teeth. Instead they have baleen, or thin plates, in their mouth to strain out food. The humpback whale is black with white on it. This whale has long flippers. The blue whale is a blue-gray color.

1. How are blue whales and humpback whales alike?

○ A. They are black and white.

○ B. They have long flippers.

○ C. They are both mammals.

2. How are blue whales and humpback whales different?

○ A. The humpback is a baleen whale.

○ B. The blue whale is very smart.

○ C. The blue whale is larger.

3. Write another way that the blue whale and the humpback whale are alike.

_____

_____

_____

_____

_____

_____

Practice Page 23   Name_____   Date_____

Read the paragraph. Then answer the questions.

In Congress

Congress makes the laws for the United States. There are two houses in Congress. One is the Senate. The other is the House of Representatives. Each state votes for the people it sends to Congress. Each state has two senators. They each serve for six years. Each state has at least one representative. The number of representatives a state has depends on the population of the state. Representatives serve two years.

1. How are the Senate and the House of Representatives alike?

○ A. They are both part of Congress.

○ B. Members serve for six years.

○ C. Each state has two members.

2. How are the Senate and the House of Representatives different?

○ A. The House of Representatives makes laws.

○ B. Each state votes for the people it sends to Congress.

○ C. Representatives serve a term of two years.

3. Write another way that the House of Representatives and the Senate are alike.

_____

_____

_____

_____

_____

_____

Practice Page 24

Name_____   Date_____

Read the paragraph. Then answer the questions.

Strike Up the Band

When a band plays, you hear brass instruments. The players make different sounds by blowing into a mouthpiece. A trumpet player presses valves to change the sound. A trombone player pulls a slide back and forth. The trumpet has a higher sound than the trombone. The trombone is a larger instrument.

1. How are the trumpet and the trombone alike?

○ A. The players pull a slide back and forth.

○ B. The players blow into a mouthpiece.

○ C. The instruments are the same size.

2. How are the trumpet and the trombone different?

○ A. The trombone has a lower sound.

○ B. The trumpet is played in bands.

○ C. The trombone is a brass instrument.

3. Write another way that the trumpet and trombone are different.

_____

_____

_____

_____

_____

_____

Practice Page 25   Name_____   Date_____

Read the paragraph. Then answer the questions.

Nutty News

Pecans are nuts that grow on trees. Peanuts are nuts that grown underground. In fact, peanuts are related to peas. Both pecans and peanuts have shells. And both are grown mainly in the South. Farmers plant peanuts as a field crop. Farmers plant pecan trees in orchards. Many products are made from the peanut. One is oil. Another is a food popular with many people—peanut butter!

1. How are peanuts and pecans alike?
   ○ A. They grow in shells.
   ○ B. They grow on trees.
   ○ C. They are like peas.

2. How are peanuts and pecans different?
   ○ A. Peanuts grow underground.
   ○ B. Pecans are a kind of nut.
   ○ C. Peanuts are grown in the South.

3. Write another way that peanuts and pecans are different.

_____

_____

_____

_____

_____

Practice Page **26** / Name_____ Date_____

Read the paragraph. Then answer the questions.

Finding Places

Both maps and globes help you find where places are. Both show you the size and shape of places too. But maps are flat pictures. Often they show just a part of Earth. Globes are round like balls. Globes are models of Earth. They show the whole planet. Maps are light and easy to carry. Globes are heavier and harder to manage. They usually stay in one place. Maps and globes both show directions and distances.

1. How are maps and globes alike?

   ◯ A. They are easy to carry.

   ◯ B. They show shapes of places.

   ◯ C. They are models of Earth.

2. How are maps and globes different?

   ◯ A. Globes show distances.

   ◯ B. Maps help you find places.

   ◯ C. It is harder to move a globe.

3. Write another way that maps and globes are alike.

_____

_____

_____

_____

_____

_____

Practice Page 27 Name_____ Date_____

Read the paragraph. Then answer the questions.

Then and Now

Americans have celebrated Thanksgiving for hundreds of years. Today people eat turkey and squash just as they did long ago. However, people use forks today. In colonial times people used spoons, knives, and their fingers. Often there was only one cup. It was passed around the table. Since there were few chairs in colonial times, children often stood while eating. But people used napkins long ago, just as they do today.

1. **How was Thanksgiving long ago like Thanksgiving now?**

   ○ A. People had only one cup at dinner.

   ○ B. People had napkins then and do now.

   ○ C. Children stood at the table to eat.

2. **How was Thanksgiving long ago different from Thanksgiving now?**

   ○ A. People did not have forks in the past.

   ○ B. People still eat turkey and squash.

   ○ C. People had their meal at a table.

3. **Write another way that Thanksgiving now is like Thanksgiving long ago.**

   _____

   _____

   _____

   _____

   _____

   _____

Practice Page 28

Name_____ Date_____

Read the paragraph. Then answer the questions.

Sea Mammals

Both seals and manatees are large sea mammals. The manatee lives in warm waters. It eats grasses and other plants. A baby manatee is called a calf. It is born in shallow waters. Manatees never fight. Like seals, their enemies are people and sharks. Most seals live in cold waters. They are fish-eaters. Baby seals are usually born on beaches. They are called pups. Male seals often fight at mating time.

1. How are seals and manatees alike?

   ○ A. They are plant-eaters.

   ○ B. They live in warm waters.

   ○ C. They are sea mammals.

2. How are seals and manatees different?

   ○ A. Manatee enemies are sharks and people.

   ○ B. Seals can grow to be very large.

   ○ C. Male seals fight at mating time.

3. Write another way that seals and manatees are different.

   _____

   _____

   _____

   _____

   _____

Practice Page 29   Name_____   Date_____

Read the paragraph. Then answer the questions.

Two Tales of Three

Two popular tales for children are "The Three Little Pigs" and "The Three Bears." Both are about three animals. The bears all live in the same house. The pigs each have their own house. The pigs have problems with a wolf. He destroys two of their houses. The bears have trouble with a girl named Goldilocks. She breaks a chair and eats their porridge.

1. How are the stories alike?

○ A. They are about some pigs.

○ B. Goldilocks breaks a chair.

○ C. They are about three animals.

2. How are the stories different?

○ A. The pigs have three houses.

○ B. The tales are both popular.

○ C. The animals have a problem.

3. Write another way that the stories are different.

_____

_____

_____

_____

_____

_____

Name_____ Date_____

Read the paragraph. Then answer the questions.

Speaking English

People in both Britain and the United States speak English. However, some words have different meanings. In the U.S. a holiday is a special day of celebration. A holiday is a vacation in Britain. An elevator carries people up and down in the U.S. In Britain people take a lift. Many American students wear braces on their teeth. Braces are suspenders in Britain.

1. **How is language in the U.S. and Britain the same?**

   ○ A. *Lift* means "elevator."

   ○ B. English is spoken.

   ○ C. Braces hold up pants.

2. **How is language in the U.S. and Britain different?**

   ○ A. Both countries use the word *holiday*.

   ○ B. *Holiday* means "vacation" in Britain.

   ○ C. *Braces* is a word in both countries.

3. **Write another way that language is different in the U.S. and Britain.**

   _____

   _____

   _____

   _____

   _____

   _____

Practice Page 31

Name_____ Date_____

Read the paragraph. Then answer the questions.

Yesterday and Today

What was it like to live in a city in ancient Rome? You would find roads paved with stone. There were public gardens for all to enjoy like the parks of today. For water, people went to public fountains. There were also public baths. Today people just turn on the tap in their homes. Roman books were on scrolls. Boys went to school but girls did not. That's not how it is in the U.S. today!

1. **How was life in ancient Rome like life today?**

   ○ A. People took baths then and they do today.

   ○ B. Boys went to school but girls did not.

   ○ C. People got water from public fountains.

2. **How was life in ancient Rome different from life today?**

   ○ A. Cities had public parks or gardens.

   ○ B. To wash, the Romans went to a public bath.

   ○ C. Roads were paved then and they are today.

3. **Write another way that life in ancient Rome was different from life today.**

   _____

   _____

   _____

   _____

   _____

   _____

Practice Page 32

Name_____ Date_____

Read the paragraph. Then answer the questions.

Big Rhinos

Rhinos are big, bulky animals that live in Africa. Rhinos have poor eyesight but good hearing. They also have a good sense of smell. Rhinos are very strong and are feared by enemies. The white rhino is heavier than the black rhino. Both kinds are plant-eaters. They chomp on grasses and bushes. The white rhino has a wide, square upper lip. The black rhino's upper lip is pointed. Both kinds of rhinos are endangered.

1. **How are the white rhino and the black rhino alike?**

   ⚪ A. They are very strong.

   ⚪ B. They have wide, square lips.

   ⚪ C. They are the same size.

2. **How are the white rhino and the black rhino different?**

   ⚪ A. The black rhino has a pointed lip.

   ⚪ B. The white rhino eats plants.

   ⚪ C. The black rhino has poor eyesight.

3. **Write another way the white rhino and the black rhino are alike.**

   _____

   _____

   _____

   _____

   _____

   _____

Practice Page 33   Name_____   Date_____

Read the paragraph. Then answer the questions.

Comparing Camels

Camels are desert animals that live in Africa and Asia. These animals are hard workers. They can go weeks without food or water. The Bactrian camel has two humps. Sometimes this camel spits. People weave its fur into cloth. The dromedary is a camel with one hump. It is sometimes trained for racing. Both kinds of camels groan when they have to rise with heavy loads. They can also kick.

1. **How are Bactrian camels and dromedaries alike?**

   ○ A. They sometimes spit.

   ○ B. They have one hump.

   ○ C. They are hard workers.

2. **How are Bactrian camels and dromedaries different?**

   ○ A. Dromedaries can go without food.

   ○ B. Bactrian camels have two humps.

   ○ C. Dromedaries live in Asia and Africa.

3. **Write another way that dromedary and Bactrian camels are alike.**

   _____

   _____

   _____

   _____

   _____

Name_____ Date_____

Read the paragraph. Then answer the questions.

Tale of Two Cities

The two largest cities in Pennsylvania are Philadelphia and Pittsburgh. Philadelphia is in the eastern part of the state. Pittsburgh is in the western part. Philadelphia is on the Delaware River. Pittsburgh is on the Allegheny, Monongahela, and Ohio rivers. Philadelphia is older. It was founded in 1682. Its nickname is the City of Brotherly Love. Pittsburgh was once the center of the steel industry. It was called Steel City.

1. How are Philadelphia and Pittsburgh alike?

   ○ A. They are in western Pennsylvania.

   ○ B. They were once steel centers.

   ○ C. They are located on rivers.

2. How are Philadelphia and Pittsburgh different?

   ○ A. Pittsburgh is a large Pennsylvania city.

   ○ B. Philadelphia is sometimes called by a nickname.

   ○ C. Philadelphia is on the Delaware River.

3. Write another way that Philadelphia and Pittsburgh are different.

   _____

   _____

   _____

   _____

   _____

   _____

Name_____ Date_____

Read the paragraph. Then answer the questions.

Tall-Tale Characters

In the early days of our country, people told tall tales. These were about characters with larger-than-life powers. One was Paul Bunyan, a lumberman. He had a blue ox named Babe. Paul did things in a big way. When he needed drinking water, he dug some ponds. They became the Great Lakes. Pecos Bill was a tall-tale cowboy. He rode a horse named Widow-Maker. He taught broncos how to buck. He also invented scorpions as a joke.

1. How were Paul Bunyan and Pecos Bill alike?

   ○ A. They had larger-than-life powers.

   ○ B. They were mighty lumbermen.

   ○ C. They taught broncos how to buck.

2. How were Paul Bunyan and Pecos Bill different?

   ○ A. Paul was a tall-tale character.

   ○ B. Pecos Bill had a special animal.

   ○ C. Pecos Bill invented scorpions.

3. Write another way that Paul Bunyan and Pecos Bill were different.

   _____

   _____

   _____

   _____

   _____

   _____

Name_____ Date_____

Read the paragraph. Then answer the questions.

All About Bridges

People cross bridges to get from one place to another. The bridges of today are based on ideas from the past. Some bridges rest on posts called piers. These are girder or beam bridges. They are built like early temples that had pillars to hold up the roof. Another kind of bridge is the suspension bridge. It has tall towers. Big steel cables hang from the towers and support the bridge. Early models for these bridges were vine and rope bridges.

Write two ways that girder and suspension bridges are alike.

1. _____

   _____

   _____

2. _____

   _____

   _____

Write two ways that girder and suspension bridges are different.

3. _____

   _____

   _____

4. _____

   _____

   _____

Assessment 2 Name_____ Date_____

Read the paragraph. Then answer the questions.

Changes Over Time

Many children have pet dogs or cats today. In Egypt about 3,000 years ago, children also had pet cats. They had pet monkeys too. In school a boy of long-ago Egypt would write on papyrus. Girls were not allowed to go to school. Today boys and girls attend school and do their writing on paper. Like children today, children in ancient Egypt enjoyed going to parties.

Write two ways that life in long-ago Egypt was like life today.

1. _____

_____

_____

2. _____

_____

_____

Write two ways that life in long-ago Egypt was different from life today.

3. _____

_____

_____

4. _____

_____

_____

Assessment 3 Name_____ Date_____

Read the paragraph. Then answer the questions.

Alligators and Crocodiles

Alligators and crocodiles are both reptiles. They look like big lizards. Crocodiles have long, pointed snouts. The snout of an alligator is wide and rounded. Crocodiles are also more active than alligators. When a croc has its mouth closed, you can see some of its teeth. You cannot see an alligator's teeth when its mouth is closed. Both of these reptiles live in wet swampy areas. Often they live along rivers.

Write two ways that alligators and crocodiles are alike.

1. _____

   _____

   _____

2. _____

   _____

   _____

Write two ways that alligators and crocodiles are different.

3. _____

   _____

   _____

4. _____

   _____

   _____

Student Record Sheet

Name _____ Date _____

Date	Practice Page # _____	Number Correct	Comments

Answers

Page 5:
This paragraph compares *great white sharks* and *bull sharks*.
1. good swimmers
2. lots of teeth
3. deep, cold seas
4. mostly in shallow waters

Page 8:
1. ✔
2. ✗
3. ✗
4. ✔
5. ✗
6. ✔
7. Possible answer: They are made of metal.
8. Possible answer: A knife is usually bigger.

Page 9:
1. B
2. B
3. Possible answer: Fido was free.

Page 10:
1. B
2. A
3. Possible answer: Mother turtles cover the eggs and leave.

Page 11:
1. A
2. B
3. Possible answer: They are wild cats.

Page 12:
1. C
2. A
3. Possible answer: People in Mexico make *retablos*.

Page 13:
1. A
2. C
3. Possible answer: They belong to the same insect group.

Page 14:
1. B
2. C
3. Possible answer: Ocean surfers usually wear bathing suits.

Page 15:
1. C
2. B
3. Possible answer: Formula One cars have special engines.

Page 16:
1. C
2. C
3. Possible answer: They have fur.

Page 17:
1. B
2. A
3. Possible answer: They are very hot.

Page 18:
1. B
2. C
3. Possible answer: Peter Minuit founded New York.

Page 19:
1. A
2. C
3. Possible answer: Toothed leaves can be different shapes.

Page 20:
1. A
2. C
3. Possible answer: They have the name Carolina.

Page 21:
1. B
2. B
3. Possible answer: Baseball has nine players on a team.

Page 22:
1. C
2. A
3. Possible answer: They are eaten fresh.

Page 23:
1. C
2. B
3. Possible answer: A blizzard is a snowstorm.

Page 24:
1. A
2. B
3. Possible answer: They have dining cars.

Page 25:
1. C
2. C
3. Possible answer: Limestone is a sedimentary rock.

Page 26:
1. A
2. A
3. Possible answer: They have never been found.

Page 27:
1. B
2. B
3. Possible answer: They are amphibians.

Page 28:
1. A
2. B
3. Possible answer: August is not a month of national holidays.

Page 29:
1. C
2. B
3. Possible answer: A pinch is an arrest in Chicago.

Page 30:
1. C
2. C
3. Possible answer: They are baleen whales.

Page 31:
1. A
2. C
3. Possible answer: They are elected by people in each state.

Page 32:
1. B
2. A
3. Possible answer: A trumpet player presses valves.

Page 33:
1. A
2. A
3. Possible answer: Peanut butter is made from peanuts.

Page 34:
1. B
2. C
3. Possible answer: They show directions.

Page 35:
1. B
2. A
3. Possible answer: People used spoons and knives then and now.

Page 36:
1. C
2. C
3. Possible answer: Baby seals are born on beaches.

Page 37:
1. C
2. A
3. Possible answer: The bears live in one house.

Page 38:
1. B
2. B
3. Possible answer: A lift is an elevator in Britain.

Page 39:
1. A
2. B
3. Possible answer: Girls did not go to school.

Page 40:
1. A
2. A
3. Possible answer: They have good hearing.

Page 41:
1. C
2. B
3. Possible answer: They kick.

Page 42:
1. C
2. C
3. Possible answer: Pittsburgh was once called Steel City.

Page 43:
1. A
2. C
3. Possible answer: Paul Bunyan dug the Great Lakes.

Page 44:
Possible answers:
1. They allow people to cross from one place to another.
2. They are based on ideas from the past.
3. Girder bridges rest on piers.
4. Steel cables support suspension bridges.

Page 45:
Possible answers:
1. Children had pets.
2. Children liked parties.
3. Girls didn't go to school.
4. Papyrus was used instead of paper.

Page 46:
Possible answers:
1. They are reptiles.
2. They live in wet swampy areas.
3. Crocodiles are more active.
4. Alligators have wide, rounded snouts.